Honoring
THE BEAUTIFUL
CREATION OF YOU
(You are enough)

BRIAN ROSCOE

**HONORING THE BEAUTIFUL CREATION OF YOU:
YOU ARE ENOUGH**
COPYRIGHT © 2021 BY BRIAN ROSCOE

All rights reserved. No part of this publication may be reproduced, distributed, or transmitted in any form or by any means, including photocopying, recording, or other electronic or mechanical methods, without the prior written permission of the author, except in the case of brief quotations embodied in critical reviews and certain other noncommercial uses permitted by copyright law.

The content of this book is for general informational purposes only. It is not meant to be used, nor should it be used, to diagnose or treat any medical condition or to replace the services of your physician or other healthcare provider. The advice and strategies contained in the book may not be suitable for all readers.

Neither the author, publisher, nor any of their employees or representatives guarantees the accuracy of information in this book or its usefulness to a particular reader, nor are they responsible for any damage or negative consequence that may result from any treatment, action taken, or inaction by any person reading or following the information in this book.

For permission requests or to contact the author, visit:
brianroscoeauthor.com

ISBN-13: 978-1-957348-05-6

PRINTED IN THE UNITED STATES OF AMERICA

YOU ARE *Enough*

> *To exist is to change, to change is to mature, to mature is to go on creating one's self endlessly."*
> *-Henri Bergson*

What of you is not pure miracle? What of you is not awe-inspired creation? You are love in a perfect form, a human form, that can generate love as well as all the challenges to love's presence. You are a perfect human with all the qualities of being human—qualities you're designed to experience and grow through. There's nothing about you that's not divinely created, nothing that's not meant to be as it is, to explore, to be worked through, enjoyed, disliked, and understood. Honor your beautiful creation, because even in your most difficult struggle, you're perfect. This gift of being you is only meant to help you further define the love that you are. Patiently honor yourself. You have been made perfect for this world.

What is it to honestly open up to myself, honestly and without distraction, to open myself up to seeing the things I'm most scared to admit about who I am? Can I allow myself to look at the pain that dwells in my heart, to see and acknowledge the struggle within me that has so many names: anguish, shame, humiliation, all the painful messages I've received from the world or unwisely participated in myself. I have judged myself so hard, made it a habit to self destruct rather than to heal the pain that binds my heart. How do I find the courage to explore past what I know, and move forward into the deepest truth of who I am? Can I do that? Can I heal? Can I open up to that which I've spent my life trying to deny?

I am the only one who can make it safe and acceptable to acknowledge, with integrity, my life and the mistakes that are mine and what is not mine. What does that look like and how does that feel to take charge of who I am? I will

YOU ARE *Enough*

only know when I try. And when I do, who do I become, who do I grow into but myself?

The lessons of your *self-love* are waiting for you to pay attention.

"Know thyself, or at least keep renewing the acquaintance."
-Robert Breault

"There are people who live their whole lives on the default settings, never realizing you can customize."
-Robert Breault

Your life in this world is about the "who" that you are always reconnecting with. Who you are in this human form, the who you are as you delve deep into yourself and explore your soul and heart. These are the paths that bring you toward what's truly important on this journey. Because it's not about money, not about things, not sex, not power. None of that matters. The only thing that matters is remembering who you are. Keeping check on remembering our heart, that's the journey.

YOU ARE *Enough*

*The lessons of your self-love are
waiting for you to pay attention.
Start with three:*

1. Free of any material concern, who would you be? Who would you become?

2. What lessons does your struggle trigger, no matter what the difficulty might be? What is it in yourself that you really don't want to look at?

3. What does spirit want most of you? Can you see the tricks that ego uses to automatically try and redirect that message? What are the most common ways your attention gets diverted, what most distracts you from your journey inward?

We're all so multidimensionally miraculous that it's almost impossible for us to see ourselves in the full abundance that we are! It's dizzying looking at the miracle of **you** in full bloom!

Is it any wonder we feel that we need to numb ourselves down, seek shade from the brilliance, with all sorts of distractions, addictions, and qualities of thought that keep us looking away from the truth of who we are? It's so awe inspiring, we can barely handle it.

Just remember, when you're feeling down, as though you're not enough, remember that you have the miracle of creation flowing through your body! You're breathtakingly amazing! You are the full bloom of creation, so bright that we all need to put on our sunglasses just to get a glimpse of you!

YOU ARE *Enough*

JOURNEY PROMPT

Spend some time really looking at anything of this world in an inquisitive way—a flower, a Hubble photo of space, magnify a grain of sand or some dirt and observe its infinite qualities. When you're done, step back, take a breath, and immerse yourself in the infinite complexity of you. Consider how molecules have come together (themselves, a miracle) to create all the cells, organs, skin, blood, brain, mind, humor, abilities of all kinds, thinking, connections with others, emotions, judgments, and love that we call *you*. Does that change how you see yourself? Does it change how you see others?

ROSCOE

Be comfortable
in your own *quiet*.

There's an art to being comfortable in your own quiet; comfortable with what it is to be silent externally and present within yourself, to be settled without the need for chatter, and to be comfortable with quietness in your world.

May the stars carry your sadness away,
may the flowers fill your heart with beauty,
may hope forever wipe away your tears,
and, above all, may silence make you strong.
    -Chief Dan George

YOU ARE *Enough*

JOURNEY PROMPT

Do you have any places where you can be just quiet with yourself? I had a friend who would go into his furnace room and sit. For me, it's in the woods, under a tree, and off the path a bit. Sometimes, when I'm walking at night, I stop at our local post office and sit for a minute. The area where the mailboxes are is quiet and still and rarely does anyone come in. It's quiet, quiet, quiet. I stay a couple minutes before continuing my walk.

List two places that allow you to comfortably experience your own quiet:

1)

2)

Never allow yourself to be kept small— not by yourself, not by society, not by your friends, not by your family. Ask yourself: who would you become and how you would live in this world when you're not staying small for anyone?

JOURNEY PROMPT

Who, what, and how are you when you free yourself to be you?

YOU ARE *Enough*

Procrastination,
one possible definition:

Choosing not to engage our lives in order to avoid disappointing the people around us or ourselves. We don't act because it feels safer and more familiar to stay where we are. However, it's important to keep in mind that allowing yourself to remain stagnant in the world generally accomplishes nothing and helps no one, especially you!

JOURNEY PROMPT

What holds you back most?
Yes, I'm asking again…
What holds you back most in your life?
What thought, situation, idea do you permit to create limitations in your one precious life?

Who holds you back most?
(And the answer better have an "I" in it!)
Now, what are you going to do about that?

Abundance:

1. An extremely plentiful or overly sufficient quantity or supply: *an abundance of grain.*
2. Overflowing fullness: *abundance of the heart.*
3. Affluence; wealth: *the enjoyment of abundance.*

The word *abundance*, as it applies to our creation and our journey, requires us to think of it with a rather unique and nonmaterial meaning— a meaning centered in the heart, and reflecting what's truly important to being present to this life. In immersing ourselves in abundance, as it applies to our spirited creation, we can no longer define ourselves through personal gain or monetary wealth, we no longer base our life strictly on a physical acquisition point of view, but we go deeper, we become something new. We participate in this world seeing all the infinite manifestations this life offers, recognizing the very breath we breathe, the beating of all hearts, understanding the wealth behind every molecule that makes up this universe, and finding a deep state of adoration and gratitude for the energy that created our experience. With abundance held in our hearts, we see it in every interaction we have with the world as pure miracle. In grasping that meaning, we open to our intuitive knowledge that we are all constantly overflowing with abundance, we see all the gifts of being alive. We understand that, as physical beings endowed with a spirited essence of infinite capacity, our existence is seamlessly flowing with abundance in all ways: spiritual, emotional, and physical. Abundance is not only an expression of external wealth but the hugeness of an internal and spirited wealth that we are all saturated in.

Walking in the fullness of abundance is knowing that we are fully and completely blessed with absolutely everything we could possibly need in this moment for the full experience of life right now!

Dedicate yourself to your choices. Dedicate yourself to yourself. Believe in you. Be for yourself. Be on your own side. Be for your success. Believe in your magnificent abundance.

Choose to be right here, *right now*, engaged in your world and swan diving into life, because, if you wait, you only get older and procrastination will inevitably make your mind up for you.

YOU ARE Enough

JOURNEY PROMPT

Spend some time today touching your abundance. Touch base with what's around you, touch base with what's inside of you, touch base with the infinite qualities that live right next to you, all around you, and in infinite directions in this place. We are but a small infinite speck in this universe, and yet this universe is meant for us to experience it as fully and completely as we can.

"When I loved myself enough, I began leaving whatever wasn't healthy. This meant people, jobs, my own beliefs and habits—anything that kept me small. My judgment called it disloyal. Now I see it as self-loving."
-Kim McMillen

Give yourself the permission to move, to grow, to kick up a storm—give yourself permission to be *you*.

YOU ARE Enough

JOURNEY PROMPT

Permission. What a huge thing to give to ourselves. So often, we hold ourselves back from being who we are, fearful of the opinions of others, fearful of our own opinion, but what greater gift could there be than you giving yourself permission to be?

Spend some time in your day isolating fear, your personalized judgment, the opinions or beliefs that you've acquired through your walk in life that hold you back from moving in this world freely, to be yourself. Identify the limitation of life and ask, "What is the antidote? What self-loving gift gives you permission to walk past the limitation? What is the *quality of thought cure* for this self-limiting habit you've acquired?"

It's not that there's anything wrong with you. It's just that sometimes you have a hard time seeing what's right.

ROSCOE

Love who you are.

JOURNEY PROMPT

There are traps of the mind that we get stuck in as we try to integrate ourselves into society. Just living either purposefully or inadvertently imparts a level of struggle into the human psyche. Self-doubt can infect us all. We get caught up believing that we're less than we should be, that we're just not enough in this world. As inaccurate as that is, we're human. It happens.

When we bite on that hook of self-doubt, it's a huge temptation to immerse ourselves in it. We follow its energy—the belief that we're put together wrong, and that we need to figure it all out, think through and fix our problems, our perceived inadequacies. However, what we feed grows. It's not so much that there's something wrong. It's that we won't stop thinking about what we're not, even when it's not true. So, we feed it with our thinking, and the thought and idea of it grows inside of us.

This needs to be ended. We need to stop spending so much of our time looking at what we aren't and what we don't have, and cultivate more time in gratitude for what beauty we are and all the gifts that we've been presented. We need to see life and our own creation as perfect, even through our lessons and difficulties. Fundamentally, we're designed to walk in and through all our lessons and growth that bring us back to our truth—the truth that we are put here as wondrous beings, created in and through love, *which makes us love, even when we forget.*

Just get tired of it already and start living your life!

Refuse to see your life with the eyes of a victim. In doing so, you release yourself to explore a deep *freedom* that flows through your being.

JOURNEY PROMPT

The first step may be to come to grips with the fact that, yes, you have played the role of victim in some parts of your life. And after that, comes the release. Let go of the victim role and open to something different, because it's through that release, that simple moment of being vulnerable to who you are, that you can find the strength to begin again. And that's where we find our power.

YOU ARE *Enough*

"The most fundamental aggression to ourselves, the most fundamental harm we can do to ourselves, is to remain ignorant by not having the courage and the respect to look at ourselves honestly and gently."
-Pema Chodron

Life is way too short and precious to spend it chasing around other people's requirements about how they want you to be.

JOURNEY PROMPT

"Be free of the good opinion of others." This became one of my power statements after I heard it in one of Wayne Dyer's lectures. When I heard this, I realized how much of my life I had spent worrying about what other people thought. I realized how much time I was dedicating to chasing their good opinions of me. Large amounts of my energy was directed at trying to make sure people, my family, friends, and the general public thought well of me. This, of course, was at the expense of living my life for myself.

I figured out that when I live my life for myself rather than for or through another, I make claim to my world! I inevitably see that all those people I was trying to impress automatically think well of me anyway, and if they don't, it has nothing to do with me. It's their issue. And I wish them well.

> *"Be independent of the good*
> *opinion of other people."*
> *-Abraham Maslow*

This hands me back my *freedom* and my life.

*"When you are content to be simply
yourself and don't compare or compete,
everyone will respect you."*
-Lao Tzu, Tao Te Ching

More light, less darkness.

A little bit of fresh thought coupled with a deeper understanding of your true nature leaves you in a place where you will have to approach life differently. Change is inevitable, and whether you do it, what you do with it, and how you do it is yours.

We vividly remember our old ways and the disruptive habits of the mind, and we also know that we have a choice about whether to participate in them or shift away. If we choose, life can change, old ways can melt away, we can reclaim our true nature, embrace more of our true and authentic identity. Of course, that doesn't mean that there's not pain associated with living in the world. It just means that you don't have to allow it to control who you are, that you can swim in the river differently now, and that you don't have to drown in your old habits anymore.

You can choose more light and less darkness, that's always been true.

JOURNEY PROMPT

Pick an old habit of mind, any habit at all…

- Act as if that habit wasn't part of you, imagine how that would be.
- Who are you in the absence of that habit?
- If that habit didn't exist, if it wasn't part of you, how would you walk forward?
- What would that look like?
- How would that feel?

Can you explore that as you, in a very real way, walk forward on your journey?

ROSCOE

You are your own *warrior*.
You hold up your world.
With everything you need
already existing *within you*,
your only job is to open
to all if its *grace* and gifts.

JOURNEY PROMPT

I believe our lives are meant to unfold in a vast array of unexpected circumstances and situations that challenge our brains, our instincts, and our hearts, simply to keep us on our warrior toes. It's as if life is designed to continuously present practice runs to help us sharpen and maintain our warrior toolkit. It's our reminder that there's always more journey work to be done in this life and we don't have time to get lazy about it. So we're given the opportunity to put some miles on our warrior toolbox and exercise our warrior hearts. Embrace it! Because resisting it may deaden the pain of being alive, but it also puts a fog over life's lessons and dampens our capacity for joy.

Believe in who you are.

Be proud of yourself, proud of the courageous work you're doing. It's big, it's important, and all the actors and teammates involved in your world, whomever they may be, are playing their role so that you can evolve into your best self—a pure benefit to you and the world.

It might sound odd but, at some moment, you will feel gratitude for all the people, the players, in your story. These are the friends, family, acquaintances, even strangers and enemies that sacrifice in the most unusual of ways for one another's progress. We all play our roles for the greater good, even though we may never know exactly why, or what it's all about, unaware of its bigger purpose. Know that there's always more to life than meets the eye, nothing is exactly as it seems. Be grateful for your life and all that are part of your story.

YOU ARE *Enough*

It's *your story,*
not your identity.
Be respectful of it,
wherever you find yourself,
and *believe in*
who you are.

JOURNEY PROMPT

How can we learn our life lessons without dealing with the difficult, often impossible, people put in our world—the ones put there, perhaps, for the sole purpose of helping us learn those lessons? Without the interaction with our journey partners, good, bad or otherwise, it's impossible for us to indulge in the opportunities presented to us. And who would you be without those lessons—those life lessons that require us to confront one another and then confront ourselves? When we take away any part of our life experience, we equally take away a part of ourselves. Your job is not to judge your experience. Your job is to learn from it, even the difficult parts, because, without those, there would be no lesson, no growth.

You are Enough

ALL OF US,
WE'RE BEAUTIFUL.

We're all precious human beings simply trying to figure out life, busy exploring who we are, and how to live in a world we've all played a part in creating. We're not any different from one another, even though we almost always pretend to be, which does nobody any good. We have little to no clue, as a culture, how to interact and help one another find happiness or truth. The best that we've come up with so far is to get ourselves caught up in the life-wrenching act of trying to understand the rules that we've made up, defining which guidelines we're expected to use to make it through our day. So, we use our creative minds, we make up stories about how our lives should be, how we should act, what life and all its participants should be like around us. We persistently and consistently get stuck in a kind of terror-generated need to create the perception of being perfect, and doing everything just right to comfort our own confused minds. We make up our own stories about being human, because the scariest thing for us is to feel less than, to feel like we're separated and don't belong. So we protect ourselves from this, we make up stories about how to act, how to perform in this life, what to look like and how to dress. We dictate to ourselves and one another how to appropriately think, pray, behave, and worship, all so that we can live up to a social bar, an expectation we have communally agreed to chase in the hopes of attaining the unattainably perfect; separating ourselves so we don't have to feel separated; doing everything we can to procure what we already possess—a knowing that we're enough and that we belong here. It's a ruthless cycle of the human ego mind.

This idea of earning perfection, performing perfectly good, perfectly right, being a perfect human, is an idea mankind has perpetuated on itself at its own peril. We've fallen into the perfection abyss, adopting a life lived in the fear of not belonging, not believing in who we are, refusing to remember that we are and always have been enough. It's a distortion of our being that, at its core, influences how we treat one another, how we see ourselves, and how we act. It's what we use to distance ourselves from knowing that we are love, and from understanding all that we can be beyond our stories of earned perfection. Perhaps our most important role is to come to the place within where we no longer need to participate in the old stories, where we come to the understanding that we can choose differently. When we free ourselves from this self-imposed prison of ideas and judgment, it liberates the very soul of who we are, it's what allows us to unfold into the world, it allows us to explore and act with a set of guidelines structured through the love that we are. It's here where we reclaim our deepest truth, and it's here we rejuvenate the courage to follow it.

What more could we want? And what could be more beautiful than to embrace the courage to be ourselves, the courage to grab life in all its wildness with our love-crazed hearts and let that be the dictator of our lives, mistakes and all?

"Be content with what you have; rejoice in the way things are. When you realize there is nothing lacking, the whole world belongs to you."
-Lao Tzu

Never allow yourself to be kept small in this life—not by yourself, not by society, not by your friends or your enemies, and not by your family. Always keep in mind that you are strong, abundant and vast! And as difficult as life can be, you're a survivor. And then ask yourself: who would you become, and how would you live in this world by not keeping yourself small for anyone?

JOURNEY PROMPT

What does this mean, keeping myself small? Going small, keeping, staying, making ourselves small as we relate to our internal and external world—it's anything we do to give in to a perceived pressure from the world at large, or from our own thinking, to hide or squelch who we are. It's not that we're always walking around like a meek little mouse, it might just be that we don't say what we really want, that we don't feel open to be our full creative self. It generates through a desire or idea, to not rock the boat in life, or out of a fear of challenging others or being challenged. We end up keeping ourselves in a place that's self-limiting and that ultimately limits the people around us for reasons whose origins lay in fear. And you end up not living for yourself—not dancing uninhibitedly with life because you're so busy habitually acquiescing to what everyone else wants.

Typically, going small has as much to do with our own self-worth issues as it does someone else's desire to control or disrupt us. Making ourselves small gets influenced from the outside as well as the inside, but we need to remember that the ultimate choice to go there is an inside decision, a quality of thinking we choose to follow. We try to compensate for a perception of being less than, unworthy or feeling inadequate, which is far from the truth. Sometimes we can even convince ourselves that we need to be small and keep everyone around us small so we can avoid feeling the pain of our own insecurity. We need to keep check on this human tendency over and over again if we want to change our patterning, if we want to reclaim ourselves.

So why do we do this? Why compromise who we are in this beautiful life? Perhaps we're attempting to please another person, look good to others because somehow we're scared not to, or maybe we're trying not to disappoint anyone, including ourselves for any number of reasons. Maybe we want to avoid an anticipated reaction, or being seen as flawed, trying to temper the situation by making ourselves different from what we truly are. As a matter of fact, we can get so deeply into this that we start believing and living our own small story all the time—we become it. It's like we've become our own worst friend. Like the Napoleon complex, we over compensate for our insecurity and inadequate feelings by acting out in unhealthy and personally unproductive ways. We might not be strutting around like bossy boss Napoleon, rather we're trying not to rock the boat, we're tip-toeing around everyone's feelings or tempers and avoiding conflict, all in an attempt to protect ourselves, but whatever we're doing, we're certainly not honoring ourselves.

Here's the goal, here's what we're talking about: Allowing our heart, our true nature, to come forward in life, giving more of ourselves to every situation. Not hiding ourselves or giving anything in the world dominion over our spirit. Finding the permission to be strong, to love instead of living life through fear. Freeing ourselves from the opinions, control issues or our fear of other people, and opening to the ideas and thoughts that we're put here to be brilliantly who we are despite any limitations we perceive. And that's what we're meant to do! We're all meant to allow the full presence of life to flow through us, to consciously be alive to who we are, and to live in a deep and full expression of all our creative capacities. And no one, *no one*, can take any of that away from us, unless we let them. So don't.

The tallest mountain to climb is the mountain of *loving yourself.*

After that, all other mountains can simply be seen as *beautiful.*

YOU ARE *Enough*

JOURNEY PROMPT
New Year goal 20_ _
(Please feel free to begin anytime.)

What a way to begin the new year!

Now, this is one of those quotes that you want to meditate on, explore internally.

What is that? Climbing that mountain of loving yourself.

What would that be like? How would it feel to reach the top?

And who do you become when you're able to love yourself, to be so connected to your capacity to know love that everything you look at, all parts of your journey, whatever they are, can be seen as beautiful.

You have to be on your own side in life. After all, who knows you better than the character in the mirror? Life can be hard. You have to be a friend to yourself when dealing with the wolves inside and outside your head.

JOURNEY PROMPT

What would you say to a friend if they weren't treating themselves well? Would you pull them aside and let them know that you're there for them, you're on their side, and you won't let anybody speak in a negative or condescending way about them? Would you be there to defend who they are when other people can't see their beauty?

YOU ARE Enough

And don't you deserve the same thing from yourself? Treat yourself like you would treat your best friend, honor yourself, be on your own side in all ways, and it's also okay to say to yourself, "You're screwing up." (Because that's what friends do, and we all need a best friend, so look in the mirror, because you're not going to find a better one!)

You can't freely give the world what you don't know how to give yourself. This applies to all levels of our self-confirmation. Self-respect, personal honor, compassion, self-trust, a deep belief in who we are, our sense of belonging and being a valuable part of this world, it all begins with us, on the inside. It's a spark within that grows like a crystal and takes its place in our hearts. And with that, we can bring what we have created and offer it to the world.

JOURNEY PROMPT

Like the old adage: you can't truly love someone without also honestly loving yourself first. Well, you can't fully forgive someone without knowing what it is to forgive yourself. And how can you honor a loved one if you haven't ever honored who you are? Admittedly, its all a journey, not a destination. But we need to at least start growing those crystals within, and if we don't prime that pump, we ain't getting nothin'! This applies to all of the ideas, concepts, colors and flavors that empower our self-love. We need to spark it from the inside, even just a little, before we can bring it to the party!

So we work our world, exploring ourselves and finding a way to mirror in our lives what we want to bring to this world. And when we can touch those places of personal truth successfully, we subsequently find ourselves more tolerant and compassionate with our own slip-ups, blunders, or errors. And let's be honest, there's plenty to choose from, we are, after all, perfectly human! In this place of self-love and empathy, you share what you have, and you can't help but find the grace to see others with that same understanding, compassion, and forgiveness.

OWNING YOUR MIRACLE

Life, it seems, was designed to be a win-win experience when you hold to the rules of love.

We are all made of miracles. There's a preciousness within us, an undeniable dignity, a living essence of wondrous measure resting in everyone, and when we let it flow forward it naturally defines our presence in this world. We have a unique truth inside our hearts, it only waits on our acknowledgement, our respect, and for us to carry it with an honor worthy of its royalty. Yes, indeed, we are all made of miracles.

YOU ARE *Enough*

In life, we're asked to own the miracle of our creation. Owning the truth of what we are and knowing the essence of our value and worth establishes a strong and real framework within us to live our lives through. It's in the strength of our truth that we no longer need to cling to the bad habits of the mind or mold ourselves with the old self-destructive ideas we've inherited. This is where we can let go of the patterned and unproductive thinking we tend to mindlessly depend on, free ourselves from the thinking that no longer works for us.

Opening to our truth is a privilege given, a courage flowing from within us. It's an acknowledgment of the strength within our own heart. When we can successfully free ourselves from the old beliefs and expectations that deplete us, it opens us up to live from a place that inspires peace, a place where we can breathe into and own our life. This is a freedom that we're all born to know, what we're designed to become. Yes, indeed, we are all made of miracles.

Your presence makes a difference in this world.

It's a fact. You matter… so jump on that love train and embrace it!

Imagine a world of human experience that exists not as seven billion people walking the earth but as a complex piece of electronic equipment comprising a vast network of seven billion transformers, resistors, capacitors, circuit breakers, and mini computers, all working together to create the accumulation of our human experience; an experience reflected in a massive electronic world. The individual components don't need to do anything except be and function in the matrix board as they were designed, and we don't see these components struggling to do anything but express the essence that they were designed for. Yet, you can't eliminate one piece as unimportant without creating a disruption in the flow of life pulsing through the whole. Eliminate a part and the circuit board will not be the same; its function at some tiny or grand level will be changed, reformatted. It will be forever altered, because all the pieces matter and we can't remove one without influencing the rest.

And you may ask, how does this relate to you? Well, just like the components making up that electronic matrix, you need to know that YOU are integral to the functioning of this bigger world, integral often in ways that escape you. Your being is not a mistake, you don't have to do anything to make your presence perfect—it's already been created that way. Deciding to do something more with your life is a choice you've been given. You don't actually need to do anything to be important. Your importance has been preordained. As you move forward in your life, you're only asked to follow your heart, your unique design. Let that heart-centered desire and design be your "doing" guide.

From this point, your choices are yours alone. Grant permission to ask yourself, "How do I choose to be in life now that I know my contribution to this world is complete simply in my existence? In this knowledge, my life is mine. What is my design, my purpose, and how will I live it? Very simply, how shall I walk forward now?"

www.ingramcontent.com/pod-product-compliance
Lightning Source LLC
Chambersburg PA
CBHW021432070526
44577CB00001B/171